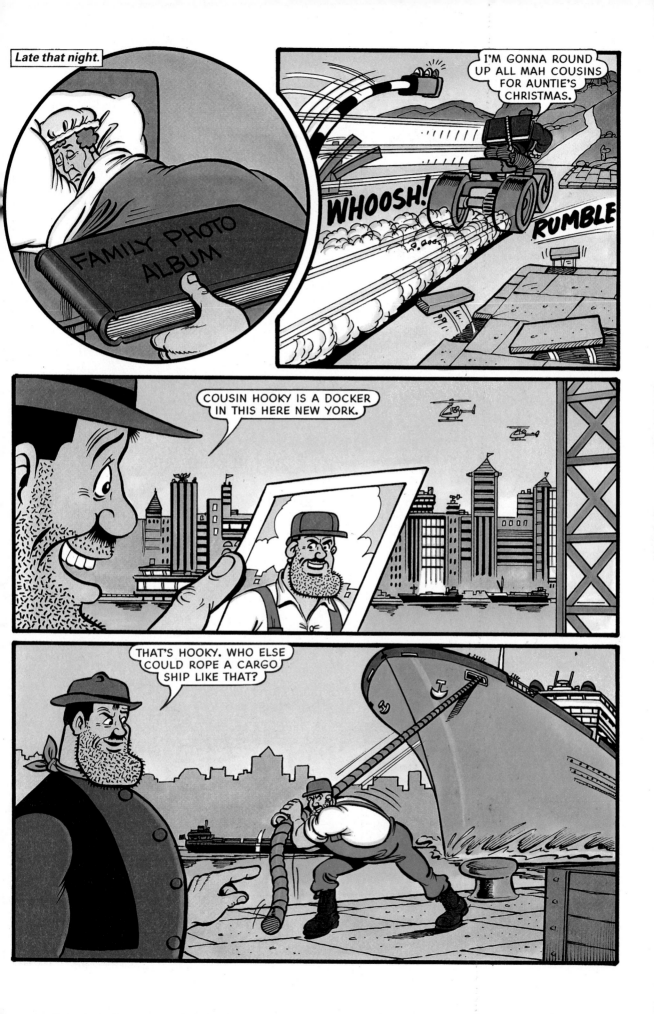

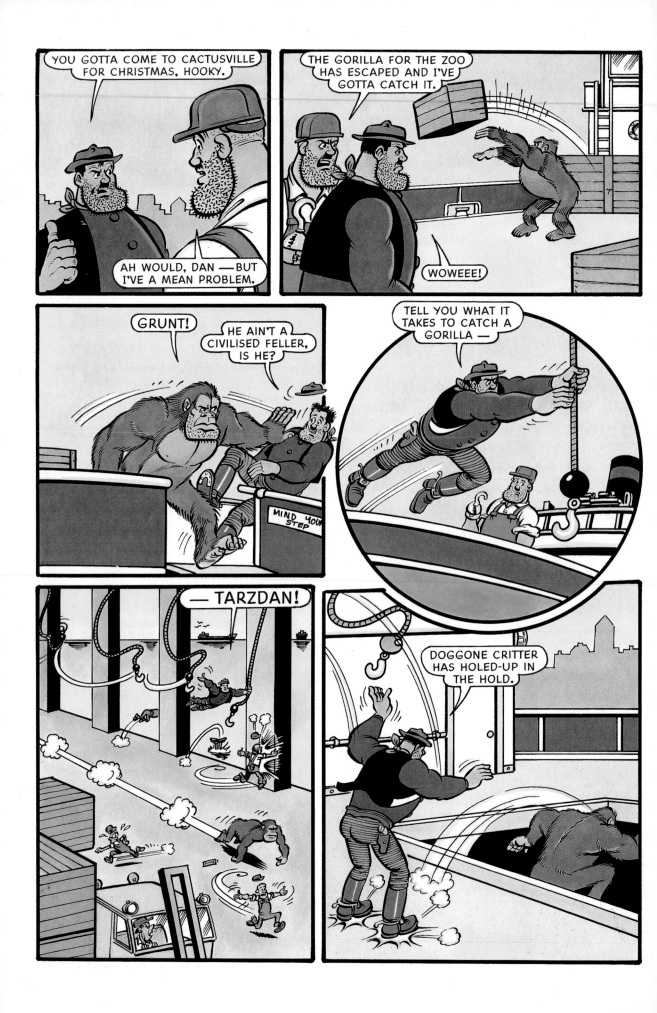

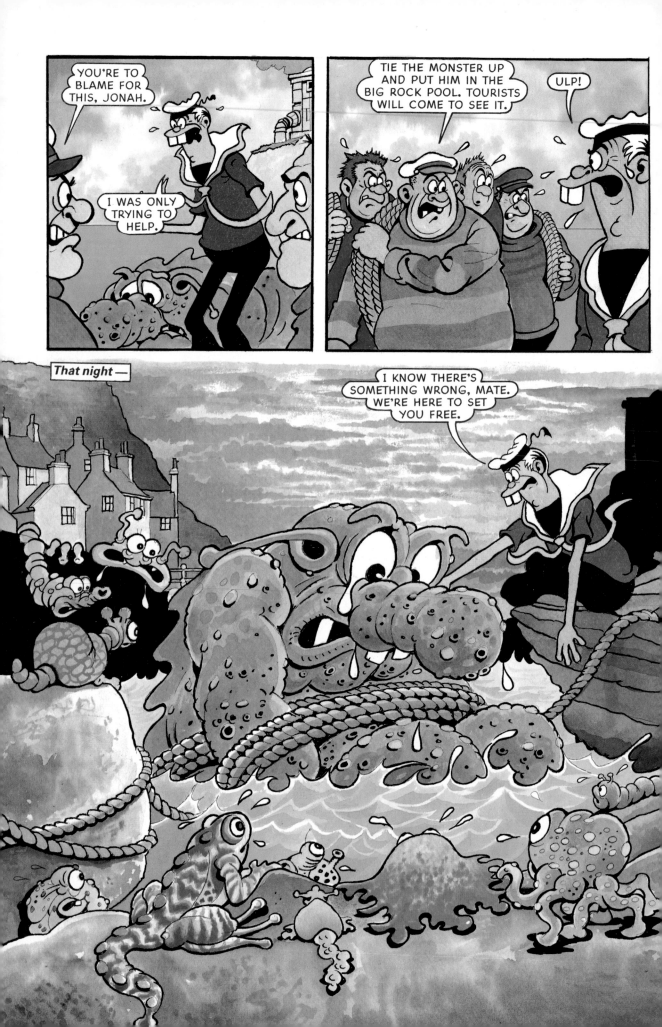

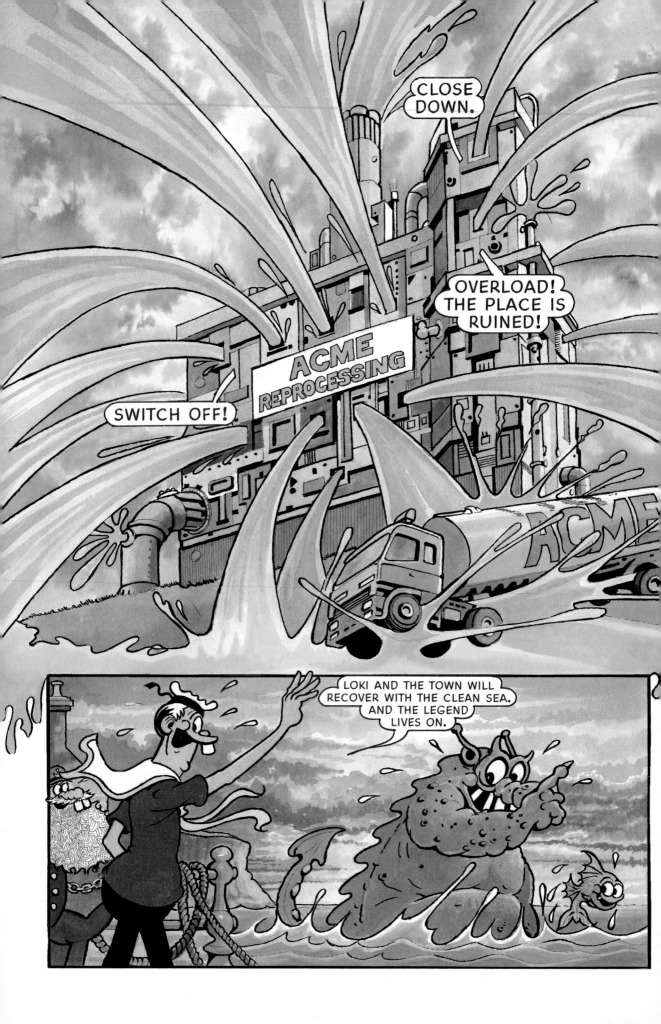

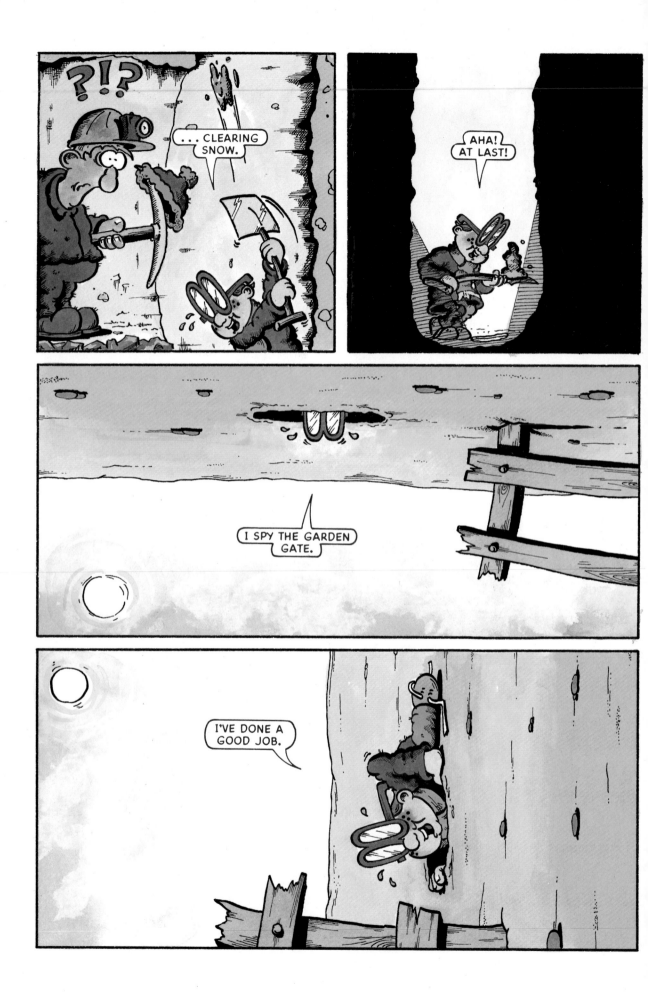

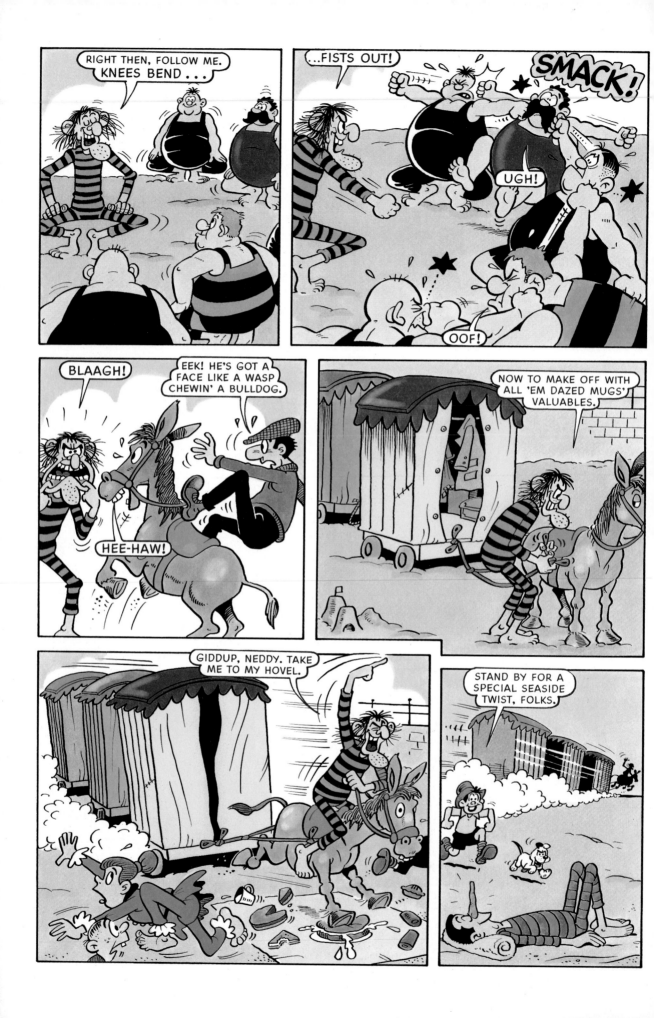

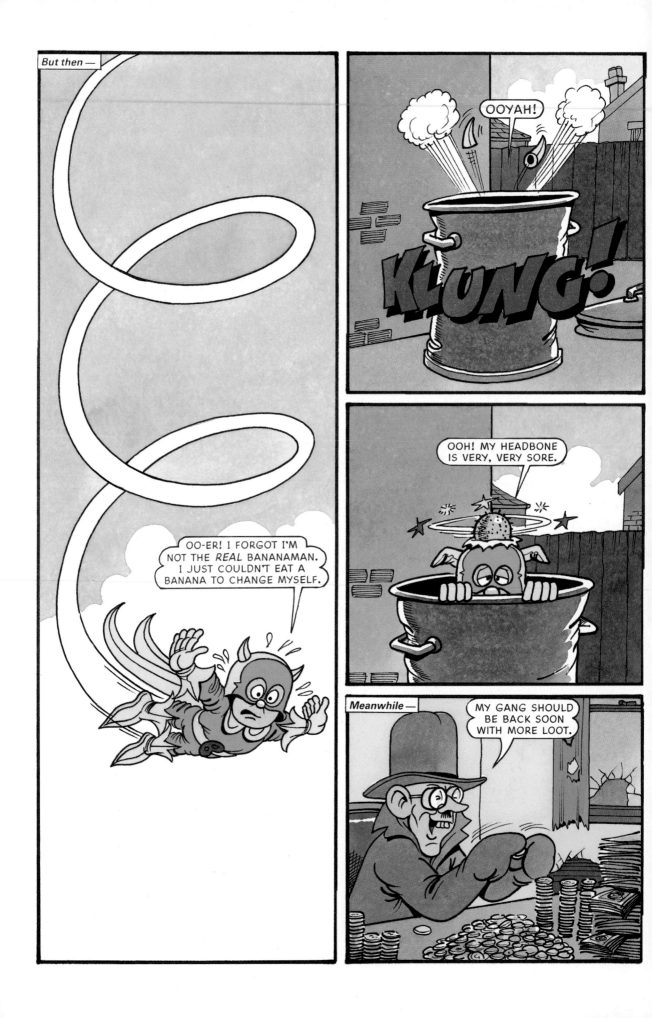

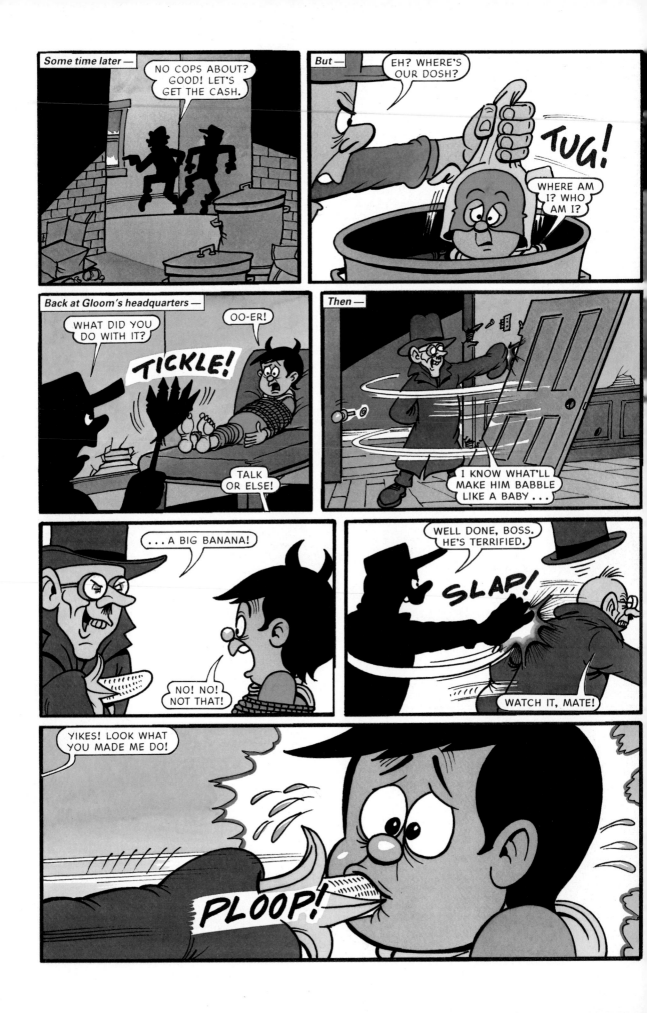

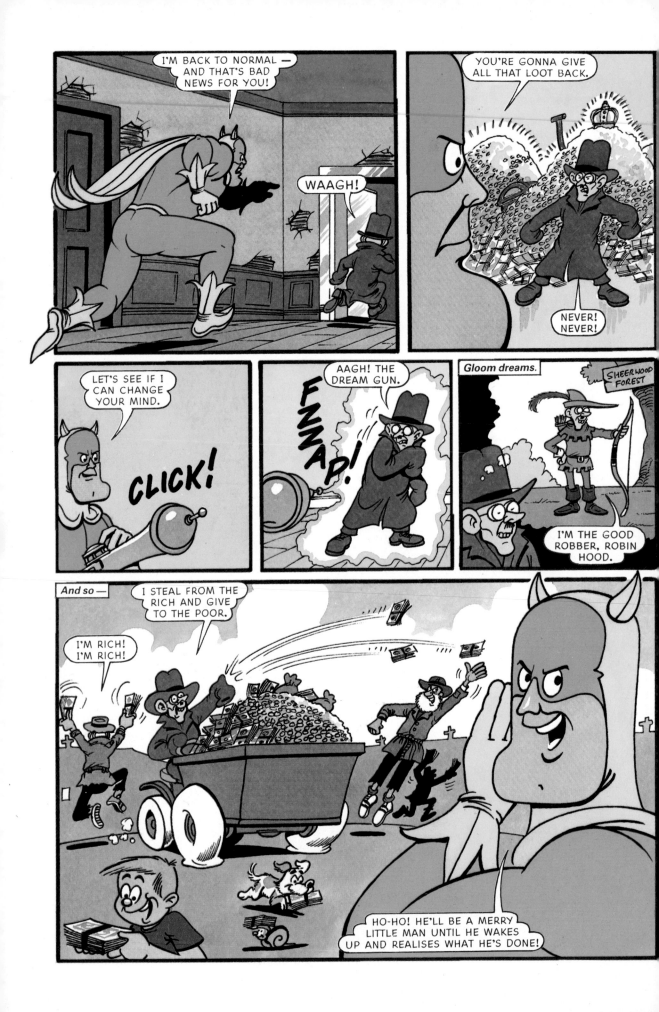

COWRIN' WOLF

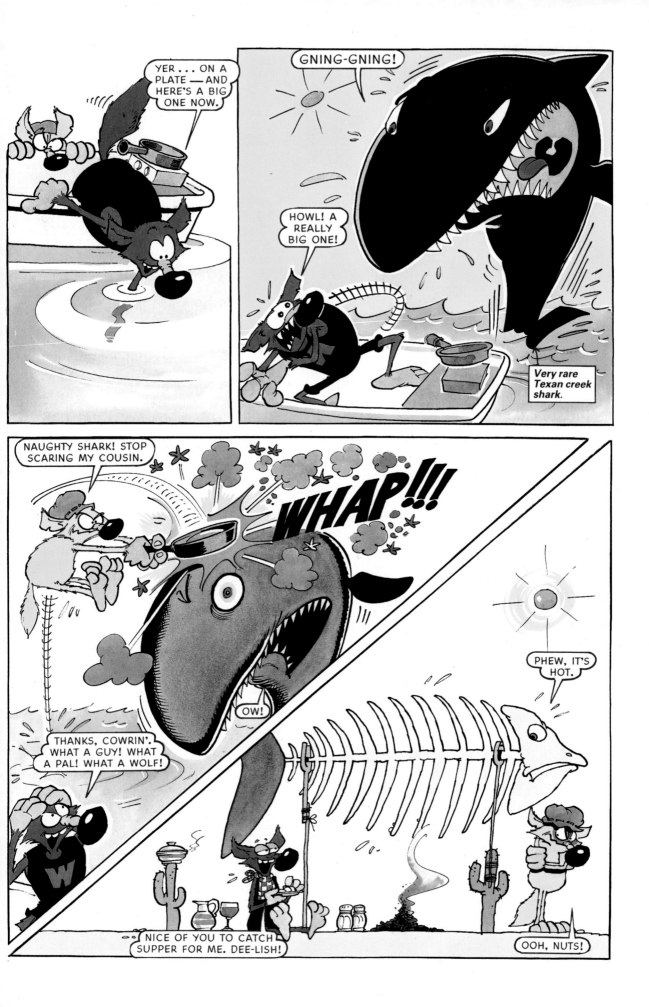

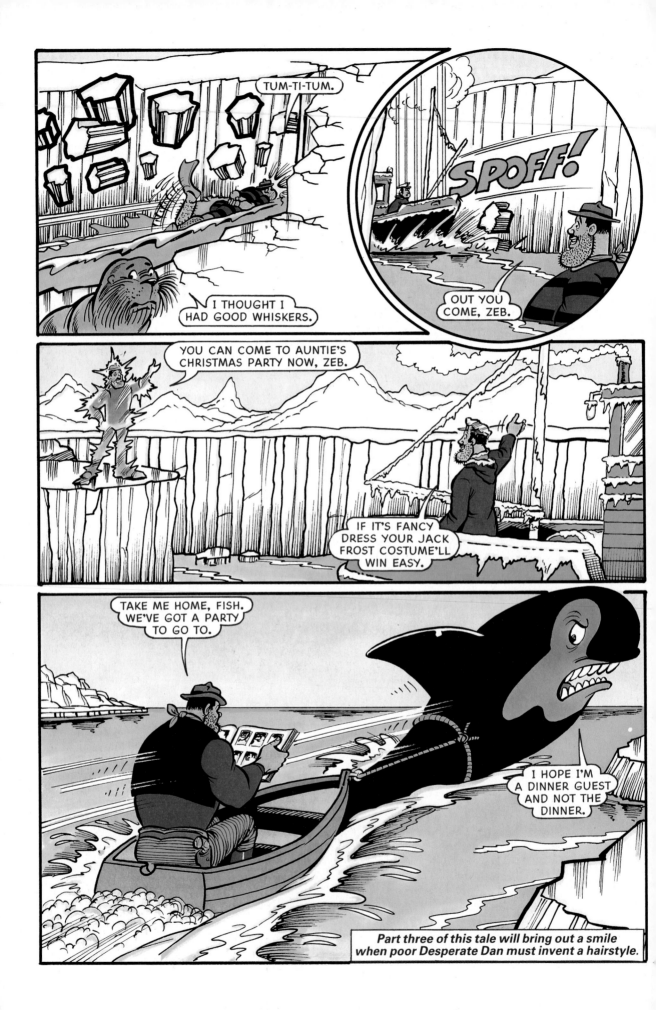

Part three of this tale will bring out a smile when poor Desperate Dan must invent a hairstyle.

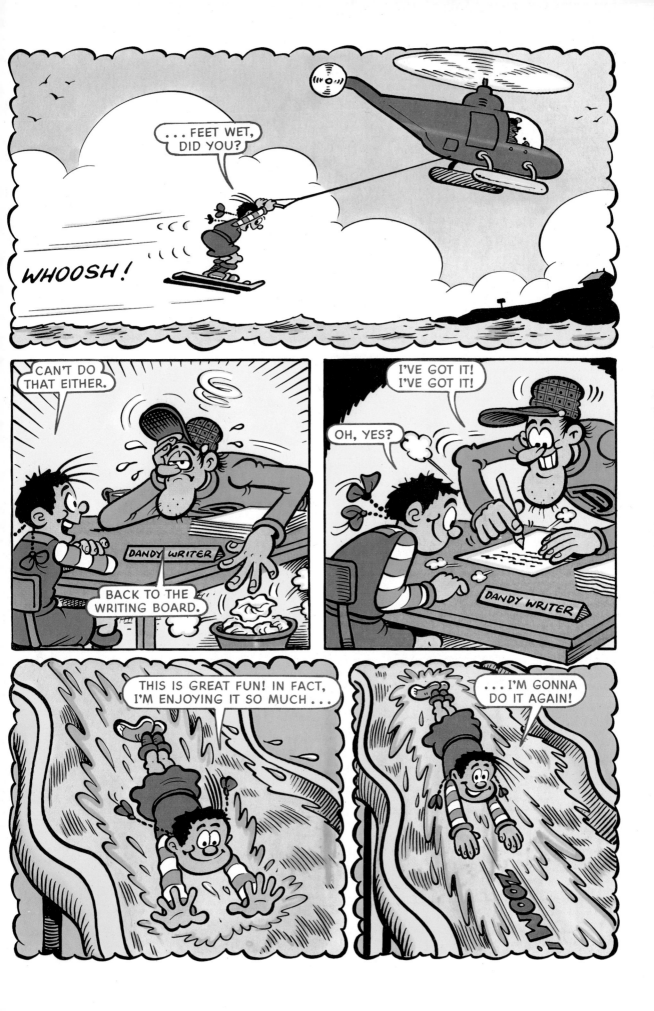

CHIPS by Bully Beef

The LOVELY MOLLY by MOLLY

RUFUS by Cowrin' Wolf

OLIVER TWISTER

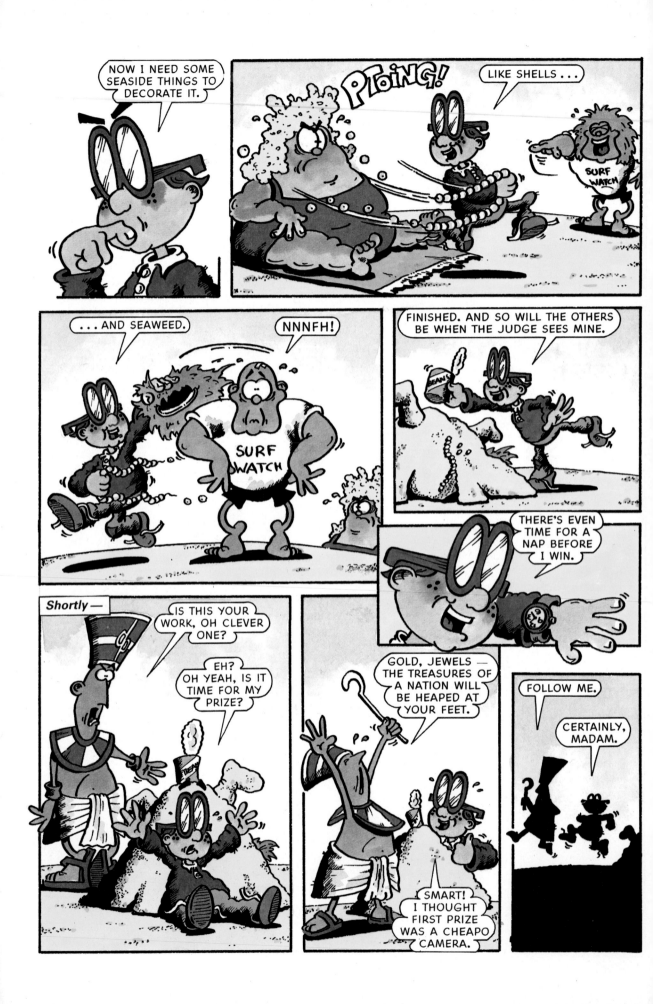

Part four of our story is out of this world.
To the moon and beyond Dan must be hurled.

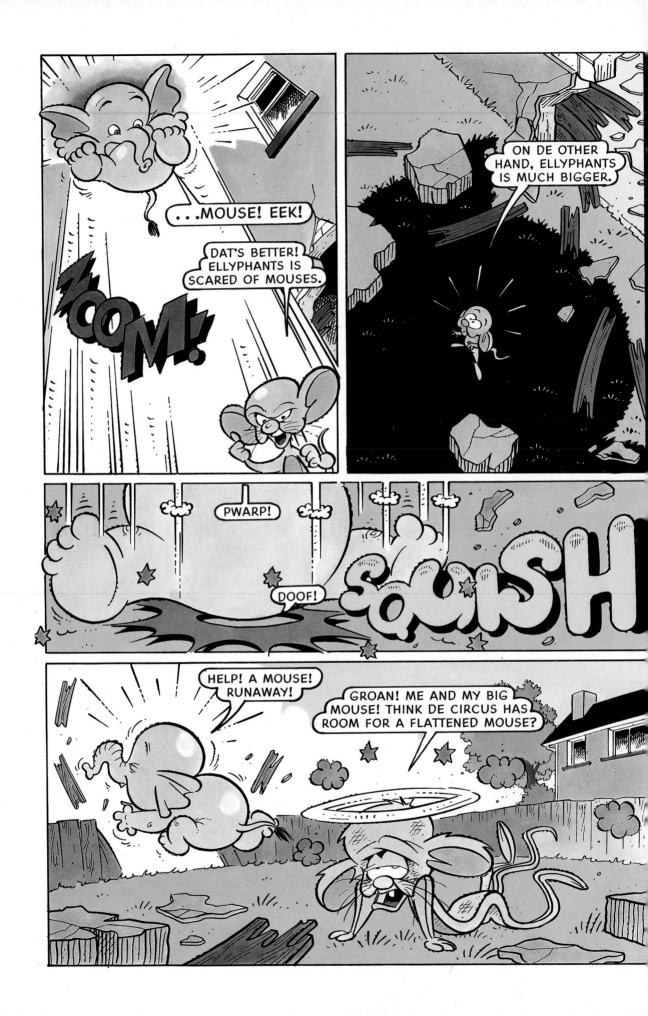

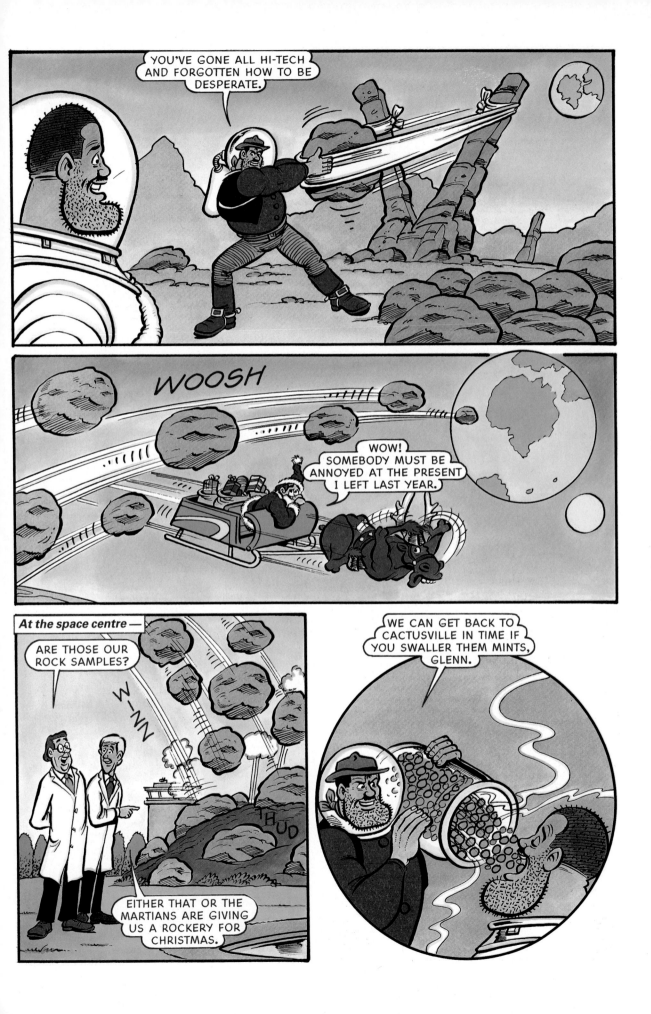

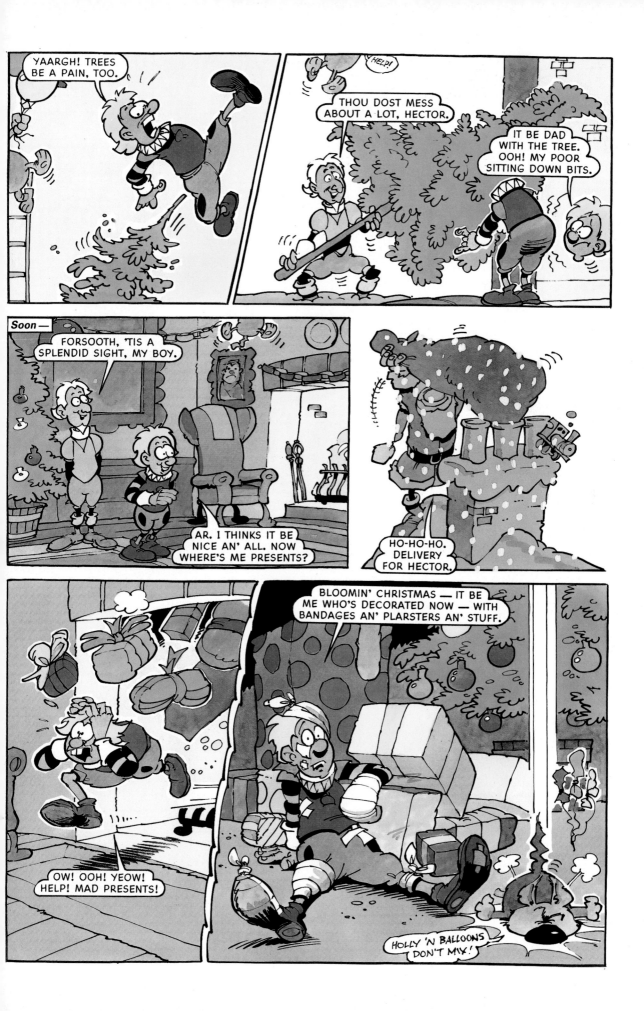